In Memory of

Francis and Shirley Brown

from Steven Brown

LIGHTNING BOLT BOOKS™

Body Parts: Double-Jointedness, Hitchhiker's Thumb, and More

Buffy Silverman

Lerner Publications Company
Minneapolis

Lerner Publications Company
A division of Lerner Publishing Group, Inc.
241 First Avenue North
Minneapolis, MN 55401 U.S.A.

Website address: www.lernerbooks.com

Library of Congress Cataloging-in-Publication Data

Silverman, Buffy.
Body parts : double-jointedness, hitchhiker's thumb, and more / by Buffy Silverman.
p. cm. — (Lightning bolt books™—What traits are in your genes?)
Includes index.
ISBN 978-0-7613-8942-2 (lib. bdg. : alk. paper)
1. Human anatomy—Juvenile literature. 2. Human body—Juvenile literature. I. Title.
QM27.S55 2013
612—dc23 2011041995

Manufactured in the United States of America
1 — CG — 7/15/12

Table of Contents

Traits

Every child looks and acts different. Some yell and run. Others swing or dig.

You look different from your friends on the playground.

What make people different are their traits. Hair color is a trait. Skin color is a trait too.

People have many different traits.

You and your friends have different traits.

Our bodies have directions for our traits. **These directions are called genes.** Genes tell the body how to work and grow.

This picture shows what a section of a gene looks like. Genes are too small to see.

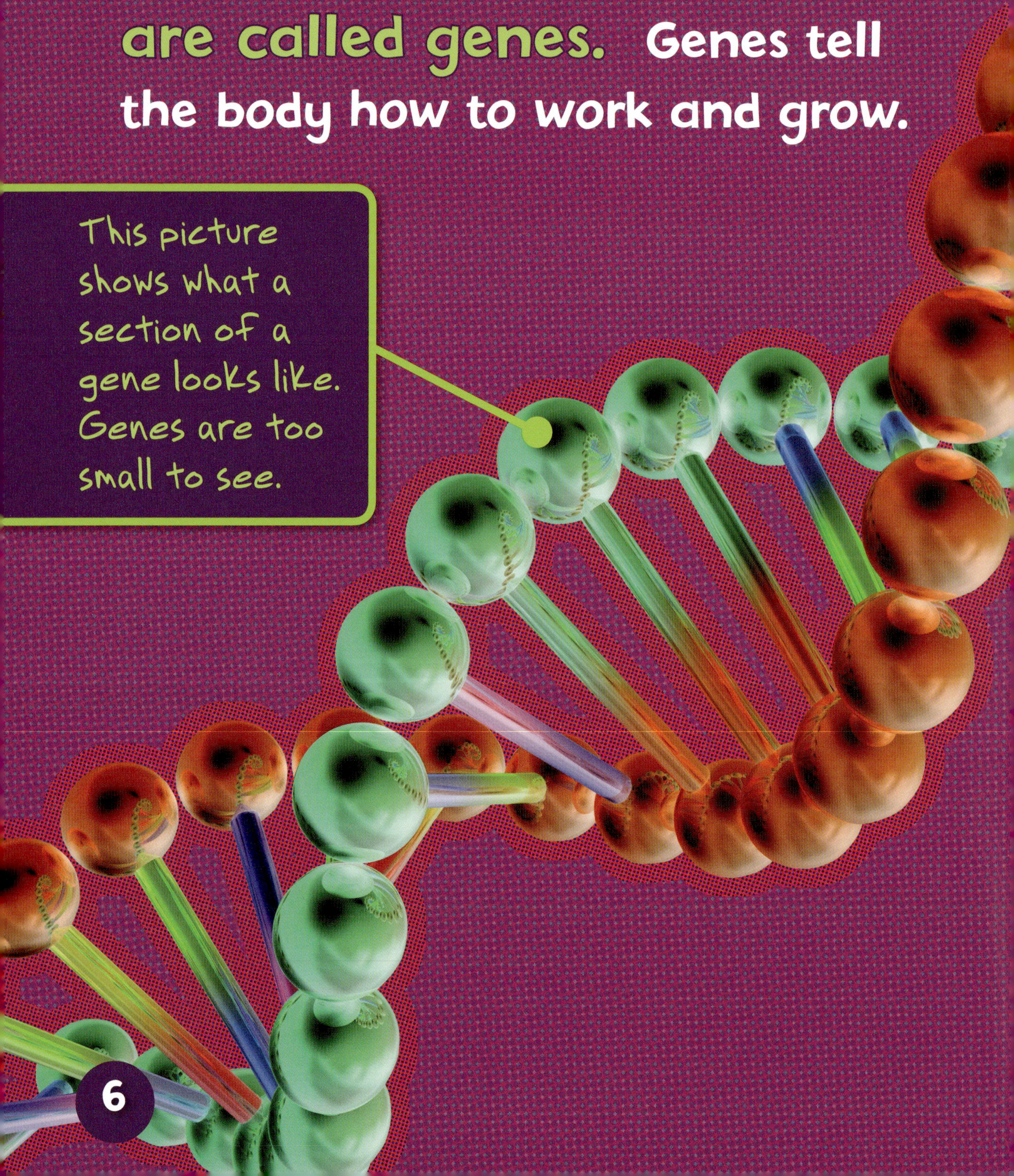

Your genes make you different from other people. You got your genes from your birth parents.

Birth parents are related to their kids. Adoptive parents take a child into their family and become the child's parents.

People share many of the same traits. We walk with two legs. We speak and sing.

Your hands look like other people's hands. They don't look like cats' paws! People are more like one another than like animals.

Double-Jointed Fingers

Your elbow is a joint. Your arms bend at the elbow joint.

Hold out your arms. Then bend them. The places where your arms bend are called joints. Joints connect two or more bones.

People who are double-jointed don't have extra joints. But their joints bend more than other people's. The way your joints bend is a trait.

This girl is double-jointed.

Can you stretch your thumb to your arm?

Some people have thumb joints that let their thumbs bend back far. Genes play a part in how your joints move.

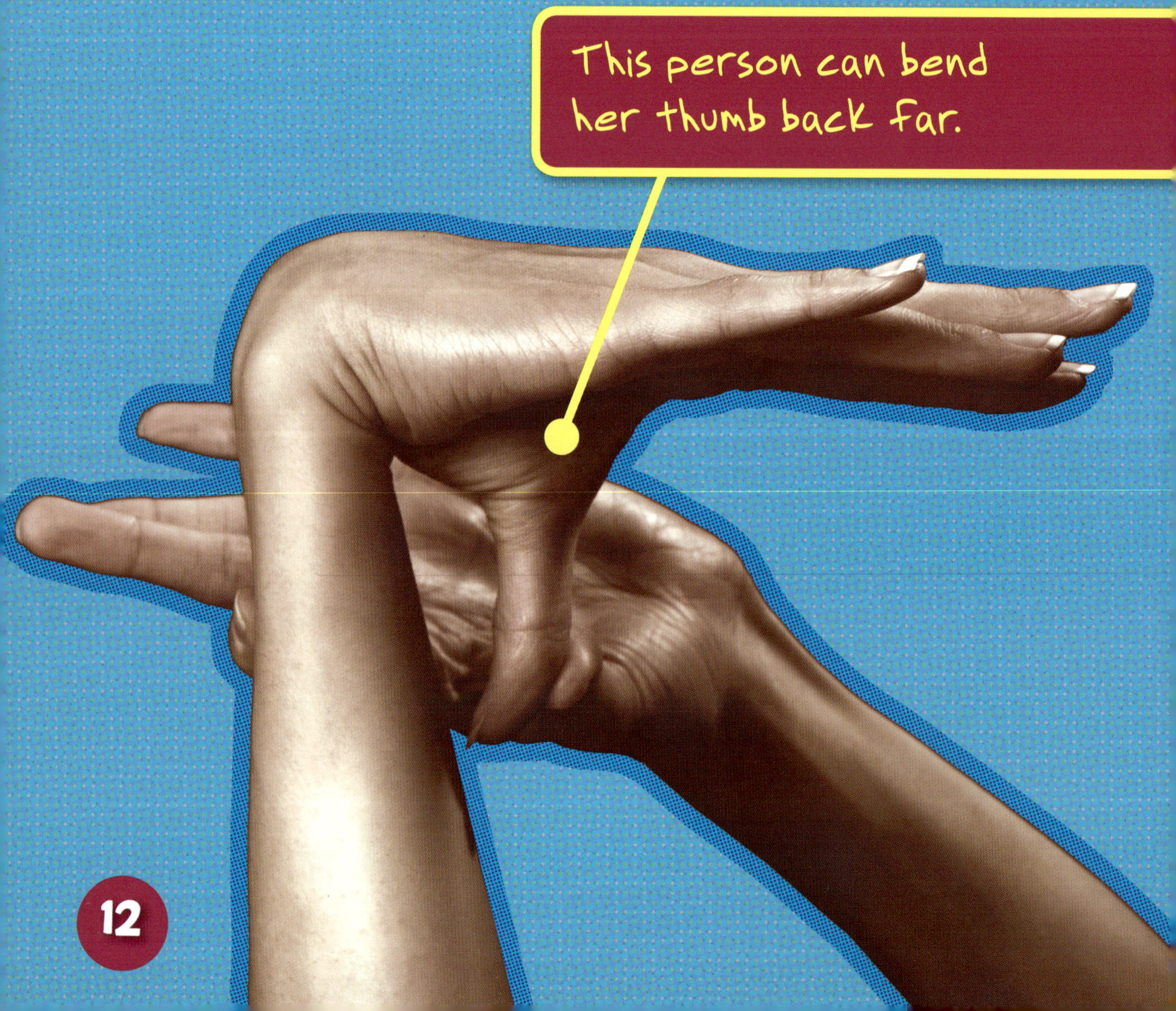

Genes come in pairs. One of each gene pair came from your mom. The other came from your dad.

This boy's thumbs are similar to his dad's.

There are different forms of genes, called alleles. This boy got an allele for stretchy thumb joints from his dad. His mom passed along the allele for normal joints. The stretchy allele takes control.

Exercise also changes how joints move. When you play a sport, your joints move a lot. As people grow older, their joints may move less.

This girl moves her joints a lot when she practices gymnastics.

Some thumbs bend a lot. Others bend less. Still other thumbs are almost straight. Your genes control this trait.

Next, clasp your hands together.

Which thumb is on top?

Most people put their left thumb on top. Fewer people put their right thumb on top. Scientists are not sure if genes control this trait.

This boy puts his left thumb on top when he clasps his hands together.

Hands and Pinkies

Look closely at the back of your fingers. **Are tiny hairs growing on the middle section?** Genes control whether hair grows there.

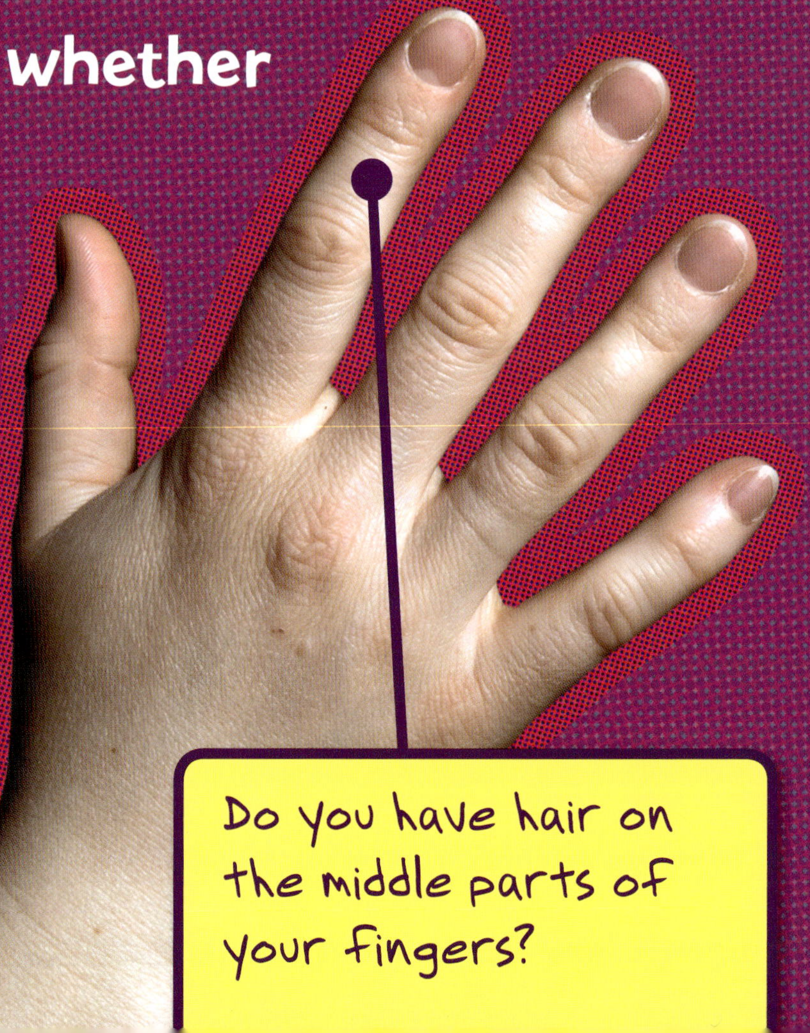

Do you have hair on the middle parts of your fingers?

Hair is most common on the ring finger. But if hair grows on any finger, you have this trait.

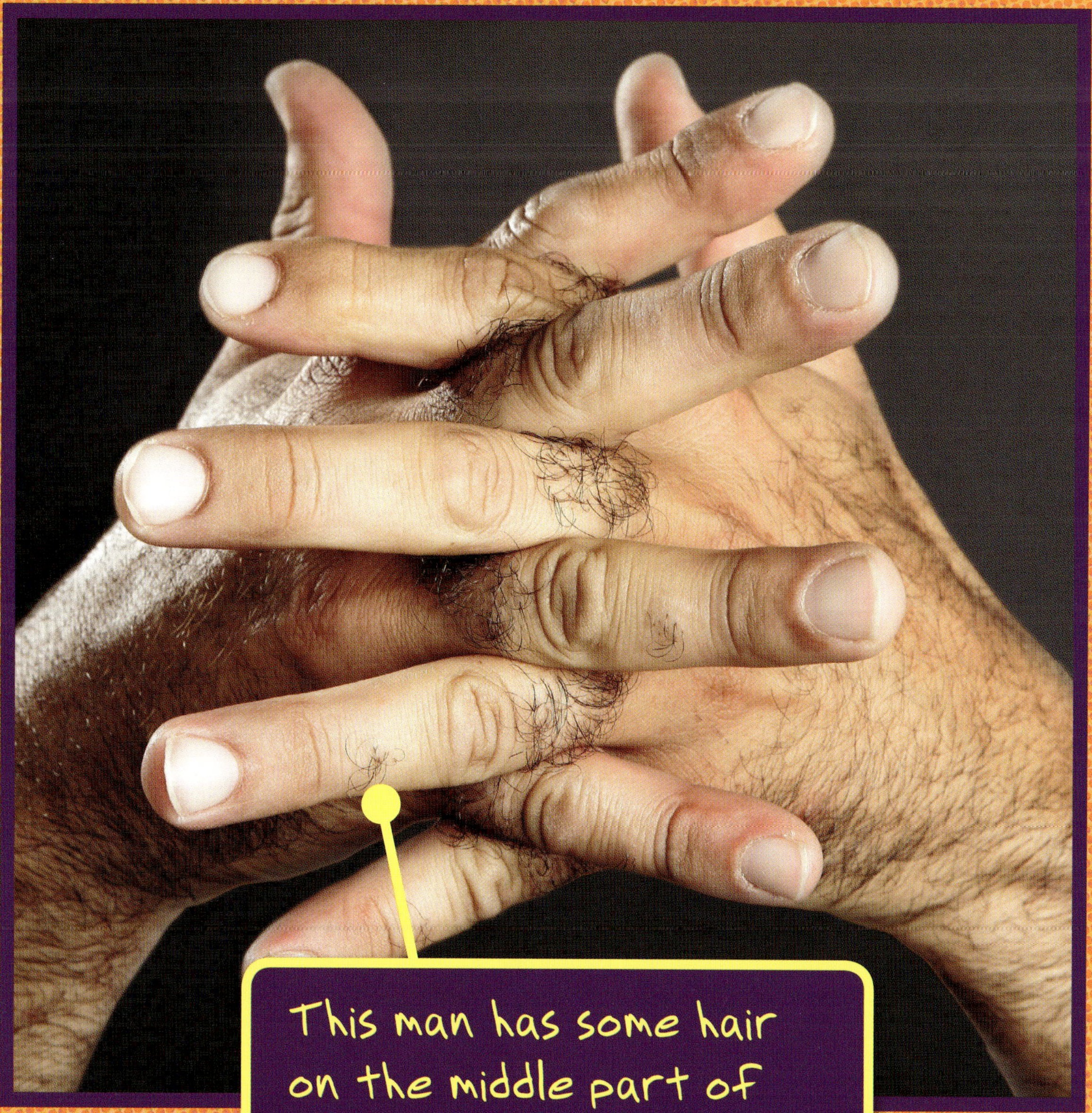

This man has some hair on the middle part of his fingers. Some people don't have any hair.

All Thumbs!

Make a fist with one hand. Then hold out your thumb. Is it straight? Or is it bent? A thumb that bends like this is called a hitchhiker's thumb.

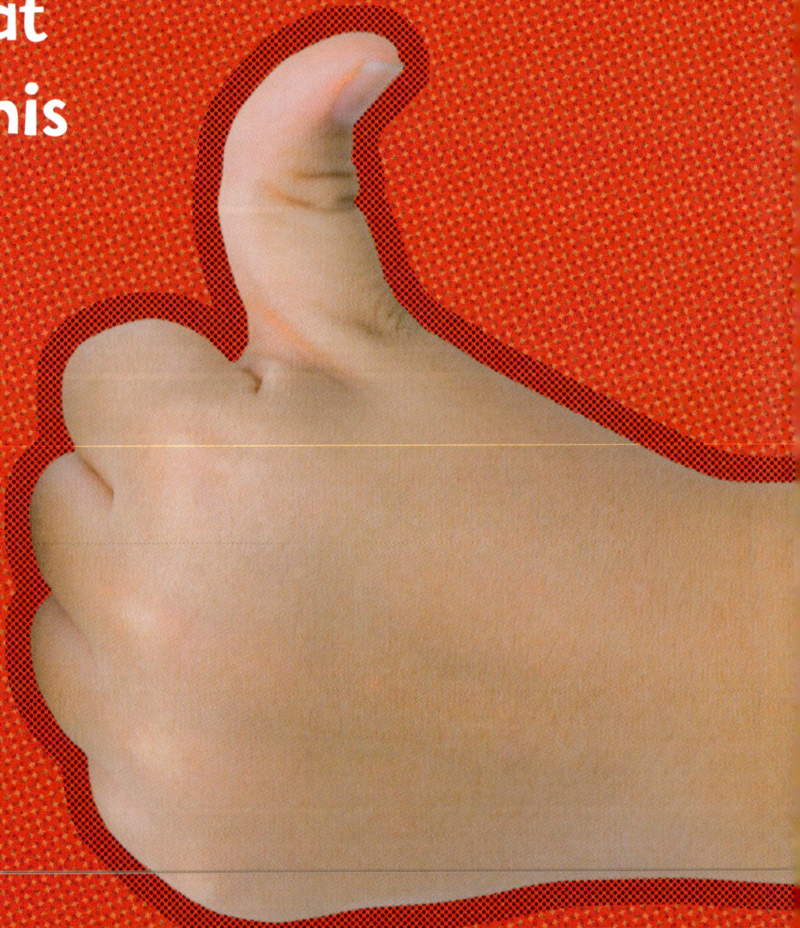

You may have this trait even if you can't see any hairs. Hairs sometimes rub off when people work with their hands.

Working in a garden can rub hair off your hands.

Another hand trait is called a bent pinkie. Lay your hands on a desk. Look at your little finger. **Does the top part bend toward your ring finger?**

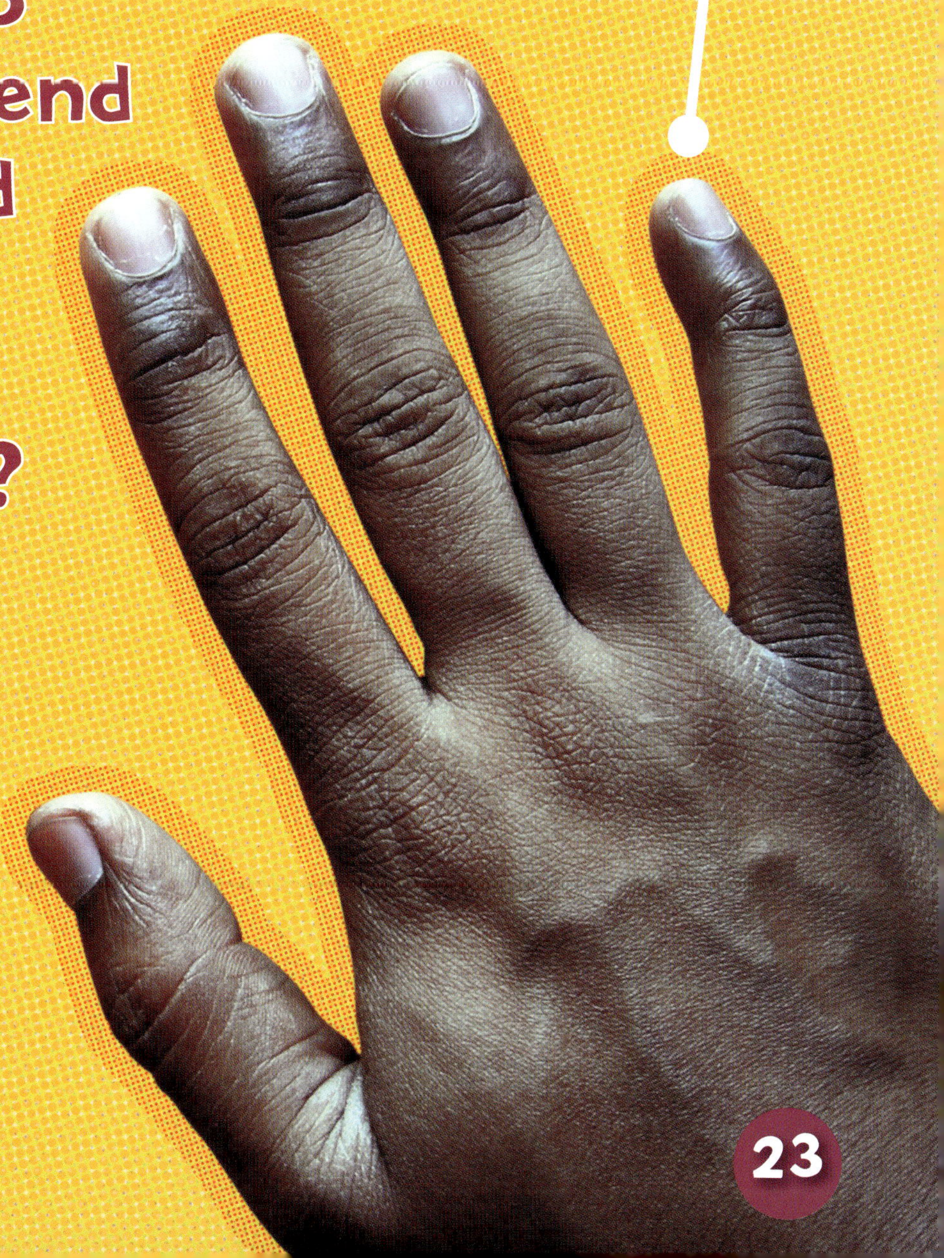

Some people's little fingers are straight. The top part does not bend.

This child has a straight pinkie.

A girl might have a bent pinkie. Her mom has a bent pinkie too. Her dad has a straight pinkie.

The girl got an allele for a bent pinkie from her mom. She got a straight pinkie allele from her dad. The bent pinkie allele takes control. The girl has this trait.

This child has a bent pinkie just like her mom.

What hand traits do you have?

Activity

Track the Traits!

Track the different hand traits in your classroom. List these traits on a sheet of lined paper:

double-jointed thumb
no double-jointed thumb
hitchhiker's thumb
straight thumb
left thumb on top when hands are clasped
right thumb on top when hands are clasped
hair on middle of finger
no hair on middle of finger
bent pinkie
straight pinkie

Then divide your paper into two columns. One column will be for the traits. The other column will be for tally marks. (You'll find out what tally marks are and how to use them next.) Your paper should look like the sample sheet on page 29 when you're done.

Put a tally mark next to each trait that you have. A tally mark is a straight up-and-down line, like this:

|

Then ask your classmates about their hand traits. Make a tally mark for each classmate next to his or her traits. When you get to five, put a diagonal line through your tally marks, like this:

That's how you write the number five in tally marks. For the number six, make a new tally mark, like this:

When you're done tallying the traits, count how many of you have each trait. Which trait got the most tallies?

Sample Sheet:

Hand Traits	Tally Marks
double-jointed thumb	
no double-jointed thumb	
hitchhiker's thumb	
straight thumb	
left thumb on top when hands are clasped	
right thumb on top when hands are clasped	
hair on middle of finger	
no hair on middle of finger	
bent pinkie	
straight pinkie	

Glossary

allele: one of two or more forms of a gene

birth parent: a parent who is genetically related to his or her child

double-jointed: having unusually flexible joints, especially in the arms, legs, and fingers

gene: one of the parts of the cells of all living things. Genes are passed from parents to children and determine how you look and the way you grow.

hitchhiker's thumb: a trait where the end part of a thumb bends down when held straight out from a fist

joint: a place where two or more bones meet. A joint allows bones to move.

pinkie: the finger farthest from the thumb

ring finger: the finger next to the pinkie

trait: a quality or characteristic that makes one person or thing different from another

LERNER eSOURCE™

Expand learning beyond the printed book. Download free, complementary educational resources for this book from our website, www.lerneresource.com.

Further Reading

Bardoe, Cheryl. *Gregor Mendel: The Friar Who Grew Peas.* New York: Abrams Books for Young Readers, 2006.

Handy Family Tree
http://learn.genetics.utah.edu/content/begin/traits/activities/pdfs/Handy%20Family%20Tree_Public.pdf

Harris, Trudy. *Tally Cat Keeps Track.* Minneapolis: Millbrook Press, 2011.

Silverman, Buffy. *Hair Traits: Color, Texture, and More.* Minneapolis: Lerner Publications Company, 2013.

Simpson, Kathleen. *Genetics: From DNA to Designer Dogs.* Washington, DC: National Geographic, 2008.

Tour of the Basics: What Is a Trait?
http://learn.genetics.utah.edu/content/begin/traits/tour_trait.html

What Makes You You?
http://www.amnh.org/ology/features/stufftodo_genetics/youquiz.php?TB_iframe=true&height=540&width=600

Index

Photo Acknowledgments

The images in this book are used with the permission of: © Vidler Steve/Prisma Bildagentur AG/Alamy, p. 1; © Borderlands/Alamy, p. 2; © iStockphoto.com/Morgan Lane Studios, p. 4; © Blend Images/SuperStock, p. 5; © PASIEKA/Science Photo Library/Getty Images, p. 6; © Jerome Tisne/Photographer's Choice/Getty Images, p. 7; © Jupiterimages/Comstock Images/Getty Images, p. 8; © Jean Michel Foujols/StockImage/Getty Images, p. 9; © Lena Clara/Getty Images, p. 10; © Bob Krist/CORBIS, p. 11; © VikaValter/Vetta/Getty Images, p. 12; © Rick Gomez/CORBIS, p. 13; © Sergiy Nykonenko/Dreamstime.com, p. 14; © iStockphoto.com/Tabitha Patrick, p. 15; © Design56/Dreamstime.com, p. 16; © Rolf Bruderer/CORBIS, p. 17; © Aprescindere/Dreamstime.com, p. 18; © Kevin Dodge/CORBIS, p. 19; © Freeze/Dreamstime.com, p. 20; © Lunamarina/Dreamstime.com, p. 21; © charlie schuck/UpperCut Images/Getty Images, p. 22; © Sameer Patil/Dreamstime.com, p. 23; © Jeffrey Coolidge/Iconica/Getty Images, p. 24; © Nathan Blaney/Photodisc/Getty Images, p. 25; © CONEYL JAY/Science Photo Library/Getty Images, p. 26; © momentimages/Getty Images, p. 27; © Gemenacom/Dreamstime.com, p. 30; © Katrina Wittkamp/Digital Vision/Getty Images, p. 31.

Front cover: © iStockphoto.com/Brenda A. Carson (top); © iStockphoto.com/Alexia Bannister (bottom).

Main body text set in Johann Light 30/36.